How To Use This Study Guide

This five-lesson study guide corresponds to *How To Intercede for People Who Are in Trouble With Rick Renner* (**Renner TV**). Each lesson in this study guide covers a topic that is addressed during the program series, with questions and references supplied to draw you deeper into your own private study of the Scriptures on this subject.

To derive the most benefit from this study guide, consider the following:

First, watch or listen to the program prior to working through the corresponding lesson in this guide. (Programs can also be viewed at **renner.org** by clicking on the Media/Archives links or on our Renner Ministries YouTube channel.)

Second, take the time to look up the scriptures included in each lesson. Prayerfully consider their application to your own life.

Third, use a journal or notebook to make note of your answers to each lesson's Study Questions and Practical Application challenges.

Fourth, invest specific time in prayer and in the Word of God to consult with the Holy Spirit. Write down the scriptures or insights He reveals to you.

Finally, take action! Whatever the Lord tells you to do according to His Word, do it.

For added insights on this subject, it is recommended that you obtain Denise Renner's book *The Gift of Forgiveness*. You may also select from Rick Renner's available resources by placing your order at **renner.org** or by calling 1-800-742-5593.

TOPIC

What To Do if You Know Someone Is in Trouble

SCRIPTURES

1. **Genesis 12:5-7** — And Abram took Sarai his wife, and Lot his brother's son, and all their substance that they had gathered, and the souls that they had gotten in Haran; and they went forth to go into the land of Canaan; and into the land of Canaan they came. And Abram passed through the land unto the place of Sichem, unto the plain of Moreh. And the Canaanite was then in the land. And the Lord appeared unto Abram, and said, Unto thy seed will I give this land: and there builded he an altar unto the Lord, who appeared unto him.

2. **Genesis 13:1-12** — And Abram went up out of Egypt, he, and his wife, and all that he had, and Lot with him, into the south. And Abram was very rich in cattle, in silver, and in gold. And he went on his journeys from the south even to Bethel, unto the place where his tent had been at the beginning, between Bethel and Hai, Unto the place of the altar, which he had made there at the first: and there Abram called on the name of the Lord. And Lot also, which went with Abram, had flocks, and herds, and tents. And the land was not able to bear them, that they might dwell together: for their substance was great, so that they could not dwell together. And there was a strife between the herdmen of Abram's cattle and the herdmen of Lot's cattle: and the Canaanite and the Perizzite dwelled then in the land. And Abram said unto Lot, Let there be no strife, I pray thee, between me and thee, and between my herdmen and thy herdmen; for we be brethren. Is not the whole land before thee? separate thyself, I pray thee, from me: if thou wilt take the left hand, then I will go to the right; or if thou depart to the right hand, then I will go to the left. And Lot lifted up his eyes, and beheld all the plain of Jordan, that it was well watered every where, before the Lord destroyed Sodom and Gomorrah, even as the garden of the Lord, like the land of

A Note From Rick Renner

I am on a personal quest to see a "revival of the Bible" so people can establish their lives on a firm foundation that will stand strong and endure the test as end-time storm winds begin to intensify.

In order to experience a revival of the Bible in your personal life, it is important to take time each day to read, receive, and apply its truths to your life. James tells us that if we will continue in the perfect law of liberty — refusing to be forgetful hearers, but determined to be doers — we will be blessed in our ways. As you watch or listen to the programs in this series and work through this corresponding study guide, I trust you will search the Scriptures and allow the Holy Spirit to help you hear something new from God's Word that applies specifically to your life. I encourage you to be a doer of the Word He reveals to you. Whatever the cost, I assure you — it will be worth it.

> Thy words were found, and I did eat them;
> and thy word was unto me the joy and rejoicing of mine heart:
> for I am called by thy name, O Lord God of hosts.
> — Jeremiah 15:16

Your brother and friend in Jesus Christ,

Rick Renner

How To Intercede for People Who Are in Trouble

Copyright © 2019 by Rick Renner
1814 W. Tacoma St.
Broken Arrow, OK 74012-1406

Published by Rick Renner Ministries
www.renner.org

ISBN 13: 978-1-6803-1607-0

ISBN 13 eBook: 978-1-6803-1645-2

Egypt, as thou comest unto Zoar. Then Lot chose him all the plain of Jordan; and Lot journeyed east: and they separated themselves the one from the other. Abram dwelled in the land of Canaan, and Lot dwelled in the cities of the plain, and pitched his tent toward Sodom.

SYNOPSIS

The five lessons in this study on *How To Intercede for People Who Are in Trouble* will focus on the following topics:

- What To Do if You Know Someone Is in Trouble
- Boldly Interceding for Those Who Are in Trouble
- Lot: A Man Defeated by His Environment
- Lot: A Righteous Man Who Wasn't Living Righteously
- Lot: A Man Delivered Because of Abraham's Intercession

The emphasis of this lesson:

Lot started out living right, but he got off track and ended up in a place marked with God's destruction. He was saved by the prayerful intercession of Abraham, his uncle.

The Dead Sea lies at the southern end of the Jordan Valley. It is the lowest place on the face of the earth — its surface measures 1,290 below sea level, and its depth is nearly 1,300 feet deep in some places. It is understood that the ancient cities of Sodom and Gomorrah were located at the southern end of this sea. God judged these cities for their wickedness during the time of Abraham, destroying them with fire and brimstone.

Second Peter 2:6 and 7 says that God turned "the cities of Sodom and Gomorrah into ashes [and] condemned them with an overthrow, making them an ensample unto those that after should live ungodly. And delivered just Lot...." What we see in this region of the world today is a reminder of what happens when the judgment of God comes. But one man who lived in Sodom escaped before God's judgment fell — Lot the nephew of Abraham. It was Abraham's intercession that saved him from certain death. Abraham gives us an example of what we are to do when we know someone is in trouble.

Lot Was There Every Step of the Way

In Genesis 12, we read the account of God's instructing Abraham and Sarah (Abram and Sarai before God changed their names) to leave Ur of the Chaldeans and to go to the land of promise that He would show them. According to verse 5, Abraham's nephew Lot went with them. Although God had not told Abraham to take Lot along, Abraham took him because he loved Lot greatly — Lot was like a son to him. Moreover, Abraham and Sarah were childless, and Lot's father Haran had died years earlier. In Abraham's mind, Lot was his only living heir.

Thus when Abraham and Sarah began their walk of faith, *Lot was there.* He'd heard Abraham's excitement when he came home and told everyone that God had spoken to him and that he'd surrendered his life to follow Him. Lot was there when Abraham took his first steps of obedience and left Haran. He was there as they entered into Canaan and journeyed down to Egypt and back. Every step of the way, Lot was there — seeing first-hand Abraham's growing relationship with God and learning how to walk in faith himself. Indeed, Lot lived under a strong spiritual influence.

Genesis 12:6 says, "And Abram passed through the land unto the place of Sichem, unto the plain of Moreh. And the Canaanite was then in the land." The word "Canaanite" here refers to the giants that were living in the land. This was Satan's attempt to scare Abraham into turning around and abandoning his calling. When Abraham saw the "Canaanite," he could have run back home, but he didn't.

In fact, verse 7 says, "And the Lord appeared unto Abram, and said, Unto thy seed will I give this land: and there builded he an altar unto the Lord, who appeared unto him." God showed up at a critical moment. When Abraham saw the giants and terror attempted to grab hold of him, the Lord appeared to him and encouraged him with words of hope and promise.

In response, Abraham built an altar to the Lord to honor and worship Him. And when Abraham began the strenuous task of gathering stones and carefully stacking them atop each other, Lot was there. He no doubt joined in the effort, lending his youthful strength to his uncle to create a platform upon which they could offer sacrifices as a family and call on the name of the Lord.

Then a terrible famine hit, "and Abram went down into Egypt to sojourn there; for the famine was grievous in the land" (Genesis 12:10). Who was with Abraham and Sarah and their entourage in Egypt? Lot was there too. He saw God's protective hand keep them all safe and His merciful hand pour out blessings of provision on them, even though Abraham was untruthful with Pharaoh. When they left Egypt, they were even richer than when they entered it. Throughout Abraham's journey of faith, Lot was with him — watching, participating, and learning.

Abraham Sought God and Stood Against Strife

In Egypt, Abraham had made mistakes. But once he came to his senses, Genesis 13:1-4 says, "Abram went up out of Egypt, he, and his wife, and all that he had, and Lot with him, into the south. And Abram was very rich in cattle, in silver, and in gold. And he went on his journeys from the south even to Bethel, unto the place where his tent had been at the beginning, between Bethel and Hai; unto the place of the altar, which he had made there at the first: and there Abram called on the name of the Lord."

It's interesting to note that when Abraham got back on track with the will of God, he returned to the place where he had been just before he had gotten off track — *the altar*. This holds true for you too. Sometimes when you have gotten off track, you need to go back to the place where you were just before you departed from what God told you to do.

Again, we see that Lot was with Abraham gathered around the altar, calling on the name of the Lord. Genesis 13:5 confirms this, saying, "And Lot also, which went with Abram, had flocks, and herds, and tents." Verses 6 and 7 then reveal a crisis point: "And the land was not able to bear them, that they might dwell together: for their substance was great, so that they could not dwell together. And there was a strife between the herdmen of Abram's cattle and the herdmen of Lot's cattle: and the Canaanite and the Perizzite dwelled then in the land."

God had blessed Abraham and Lot so immensely that the one parcel of land they were trying to live on could no longer comfortably hold all their possessions. There was an overflow of sheep, cattle, gold, silver, and servants. Tents upon tents were erected everywhere, and there was just not enough room. Tension between Abraham's and Lot's employees turned into strife. Abraham recognized it and immediately took action.

And Abram said unto Lot, Let there be no strife, I pray thee, between me and thee, and between my herdmen and thy herdmen; for we be brethren. Is not the whole land before thee? separate thyself, I pray thee, from me: if thou wilt take the left hand, then I will go to the right; or if thou depart to the right hand, then I will go to the left.

— Genesis 13:8,9

Here we see that Abraham took the lead as the patriarch of the family and exercised his spiritual authority, and Lot was in submission to him. At that point, the strife was not between Abraham and Lot; it was between their workers. Abraham didn't want things to escalate and turn bitter between him and Lot. After all, they were relatives, and Abraham saw Lot as his only possible heir. Thus, Abraham suggested they separate from each other, and he gave Lot first choice of the land.

Lot's First Independent Choice Was Not a Good One

The Bible says, "Lot lifted up his eyes, and beheld all the plain of Jordan, that it was well watered every where, before the Lord destroyed Sodom and Gomorrah, even as the garden of the Lord, like the land of Egypt, as thou comest unto Zoar" (Genesis 13:10). From Lot's vantagepoint, he could see the entire region. The Scripture says he "beheld" it, which means *to scrutinize; to view with delight*. Verse 11 adds, "Then Lot chose him all the plain of Jordan; and Lot journeyed east: and they separated themselves the one from the other." This was Lot's first independent choice, and it was not a good one.

Think about it. Lot had walked with God, experienced God's divine protection and abundant blessings, stood in faith, and called upon the Lord. Yet he allowed the alluring appeal of Sodom to draw him away from God. If he would have been wise, he would have told Abraham, "I'm going to stay right here. I like being under your spiritual covering and influence. The favor of God is on you, and when I'm near you, I'm blessed too." But that is not what Lot did. He walked by sight instead of by faith and chose to separate from Abraham. It was all downhill from there.

Lot's decision revealed a lot about his character. Remember, he was from Ur of the Chaldeans, and although he had left Ur, it appears Ur never left him. Abraham had had a dramatic encounter with God that led to his conversion, but there is no evidence in Scripture showing that Lot had a similar experience — only that he was following his uncle on his journey.

We often see situations like this in our homes. One or both parents experience a life-transforming encounter with Jesus, and they raise their children in church and in accordance with God's Word. Yet their children don't experience the same kind of encounter their parents did, so the lure of the world is stronger and more appealing in their lives. Eventually, they end smack dab in the middle of sin, in desperate need of Jesus' merciful intervention.

Lot Pitched His Tent Toward Sodom

It's important to see what Lot chose and what did Abraham chose. The Scripture says, "Abram dwelled in the land of Canaan, and Lot dwelled in the cities of the plain, and pitched his tent toward Sodom" (Genesis 13:12). Canaan was the land of promise; thus Abraham chose to remain living in the promises of God. Lot, on the other hand, "pitched his tent toward Sodom."

The phrase "pitched his tent" means he was *focused in the direction of Sodom.* In the evening, he could see the lights of the city and hear its sounds in the distance. It's possible that he could smell the city's odors wafting through the air, and this was all observed and taken in by Lot as he sat within the comfort of his tent. Little by little, the sensuality of Sodom drew him closer and closer until he was living right in the midst of the city itself.

This is a picture of how sin works. People who have been raised in the right way don't rush into sin. It's usually a gradual descent, one step at a time. Little by little, they talk themselves into backsliding. They convince themselves that it's okay for them to leave where they are and move toward a place of compromise — completely overlooking the potentially deadly consequences that will accompany their decision.

"Why would someone do that?" you might ask. Well, let's look at why Lot did it.

The journey of faith that Lot had endured with Abraham had been very difficult at times. It required a great deal of trust in God, and it wasn't always enjoyable or comfortable. He had traipsed through the barren wilderness, endured inconveniences and difficulties, suffered famine, and faced the dangers of Canaanite giants, etc. — and it appears Lot was just tired of it. Sodom appeared to be a city of opulence and opportunity. It featured fabulous entertainment and offered so many exciting experiences that he eventually relocated there and raised his family in that wicked environment.

Friend, you need to realize that your walk of faith will sometimes be quite challenging. The magnetic pull of the world and the delusive glamor of sin can be very appealing, but don't take the bait. It is a well-orchestrated lie. Worldly pleasures are fleeting, and the end results are death and destruction (*see* Proverbs 14:12; Hebrews 11:25). Lot exchanged the life of faith with Abraham for the short-lived pleasures of Sodom. His conscience became seared, and it eventually destroyed his whole family.

If someone you know is on the verge of making this mistake, it's time to intercede for them in prayer.

STUDY QUESTIONS

Study to shew thyself approved unto God, a workman that needeth not to be ashamed, rightly dividing the word of truth.
— 2 Timothy 2:15

1. What new insights have you learned about Lot, Abraham, their relationship with each other, and their individual relationships with God?
2. Strife is an undercurrent of anger that can develop in relationships and cause major devastation if not dealt with. According to Proverbs 17:14 and 18:19, what are the dangers of allowing strife to go unchecked between you and those you love?
3. The greatest antidote for the poison of strife is *love*. First Corinthians 13:4-8 paints a picture of God's love toward you and the kind of love He wants to flow through you toward others. After reading this passage, what would you say love looks like?

PRACTICAL APPLICATION

But be ye doers of the word, and not hearers only, deceiving your own selves.
— James 1:22

1. Abraham was a strong spiritual influence in Lot's life. As they did life together, Lot could see firsthand what it looked like to walk in faith, worship the Lord, and come through difficult circumstances. Who in your life has been like Abraham to you? What have been the most impactful lessons you have learned from observing this person's life?

2. Lot had walked with God, experienced God's divine protection and abundant blessings, stood in faith, and called upon the Lord. Yet he allowed the alluring appeal of Sodom to draw him away from God. Be honest. Is there something ungodly trying to draw you away from your relationship with God? If so, what is it?

3. Proverbs 5:8 *AMPC* urges us to "…avoid the very scenes of temptation." What can you learn from Lot's poor choice and apply in your own life to avoid the scenes of temptation and the painful results that come with succumbing to temptation?

LESSON 2

TOPIC

Boldly Interceding for Those Who Are in Trouble

SCRIPTURES

1. **Genesis 13:10-13** — And Lot lifted up his eyes, and beheld all the plain of Jordan, that it was well watered every where, before the Lord destroyed Sodom and Gomorrah, even as the garden of the Lord, like the land of Egypt, as thou comest unto Zoar. Then Lot chose him all the plain of Jordan; and Lot journeyed east: and they separated themselves the one from the other. Abram dwelled in the land of Canaan, and Lot dwelled in the cities of the plain, and pitched his tent toward Sodom. But the men of Sodom were wicked and sinners before the Lord exceedingly.

2. **Genesis 18:1,2** — And the Lord appeared unto him in the plains of Mamre: and he sat in the tent door in the heat of the day. And he lift up his eyes and looked, and, lo, three men stood by him: and when he

saw them, he ran to meet them from the tent door, and bowed himself toward the ground.

3. **Genesis 18:16,17** — And the men rose up from thence, and looked toward Sodom: and Abraham went with them to bring them on the way. And the Lord said, Shall I hide from Abraham that thing which I do?

4. **Genesis 18:20-33** — And the Lord said, Because the cry of Sodom and Gomorrah is great, and because their sin is very grievous, I will go down now, and see whether they have done altogether according to the cry of it, which is come unto me; and if not, I will know. And the men turned their faces from thence, and went toward Sodom: but Abraham stood yet before the Lord. And Abraham drew near, and said, Wilt thou also destroy the righteous with the wicked? Peradventure there be fifty righteous within the city: wilt thou also destroy and not spare the place for the fifty righteous that are therein? That be far from thee to do after this manner, to slay the righteous with the wicked: and that the righteous should be as the wicked, that be far from thee: Shall not the Judge of all the earth do right? And the Lord said, If I find in Sodom fifty righteous within the city, then I will spare all the place for their sakes. And Abraham answered and said, Behold now, I have taken upon me to speak unto the Lord, which am but dust and ashes. Peradventure there shall lack five of the fifty righteous: wilt thou destroy all the city for lack of five? And he said, If I find there forty and five, I will not destroy it. And he spake unto him yet again, and said, Peradventure there shall be forty found there. And he said, I will not do it for forty's sake. And he said unto him, Oh let not the Lord be angry, and I will speak: Peradventure there shall thirty be found there. And he said, I will not do it, if I find thirty there. And he said, Behold now, I have taken upon me to speak unto the Lord: Peradventure there shall be twenty found there. And he said, I will not destroy it for twenty's sake. And he said, Oh let not the Lord be angry, and I will speak yet but this once: Peradventure ten shall be found there. And he said, I will not destroy it for ten's sake. And the Lord went his way, as soon as he had left communing with Abraham: and Abraham returned unto his place.

5. **Hebrews 4:16** — Let us therefore come boldly unto the throne of grace, that we may obtain mercy, and find grace to help in time of need.

GREEK WORDS

1. "boldly" — παρρησία (*parresia*): used in ancient times to depict one who speaks his mind and who does it straightforwardly and with great confidence

2. "help in time of need" — βοήθεια (*boetheia*): pictures helping a person with his or her needs; first and foremost, it was an early military word that depicted the moment when a soldier heard a fellow fighter was entrenched in battle, captured, or struggling — and once alerted to this situation, the soldier quickly went into battle to fight for the safety and well-being of his fellow fighter who was in trouble

SYNOPSIS

The southern end of the Dead Sea marks the location of the renowned cities of Sodom and Gomorrah. In the days of the patriarchs, the soil of these cities was exceedingly fertile, and the population was exceedingly large. At the same time, the people who lived there were extremely wicked. In fact, the sin that was taking place was so grievous, its sound could be heard in the throne room of Heaven.

Accompanied by two angels, Jesus came to earth in pre-incarnate form to see for Himself if the sin of these cities was as wicked as the cry He was hearing in Heaven. Out of great concern for Lot, Abraham stood before the Lord and began boldly interceding for his nephew and his family. Indeed, Lot would have perished in Sodom's judgment had it not been for Abraham's prayers.

The emphasis of this lesson:

Just as Abraham boldly interceded for his nephew Lot, *you* can boldly intercede for those who are in trouble. Your prayers are powerful and can move the heart of God to rescue those who are unaware that they are in danger.

Lot Had a Great Beginning

As we learned in our last lesson, when Abraham and Sarah began their walk of faith, their nephew Lot was with them. When Abraham announced his conversion after God had spoken to him and initiated a loving relationship with Abraham, Lot was there. When Abraham took Sarah and all his possessions and left Haran, Lot went with them.

When Abraham entered the land of Canaan and saw the giants living there, Lot was there. Lot not only saw the giants, he also saw his uncle's response to the situation. Rather than seeing Abraham run in fear, Lot watched as Abraham heard the voice of God and was strengthened by His promises.

To commemorate the Lord's appearance and to thank Him for His promises, Abraham built an altar and worshiped the Lord. And who was there assisting in building the altar and participating in worship? You probably guessed it — it was Lot! He was also there when Abraham and Sarah went down to Egypt during the famine. He observed as God's hand protected them and abundantly blessed them with livestock, servants, and precious possessions.

You might say Lot and Abraham had a parallel walk of faith during those early years. Everywhere one went, the other went too. All the blessings that Abraham received overflowed into Lot's life as well. Without question, Lot was in a good place under a strong, healthy spiritual influence.

Lot Looked Toward Sodom
While Abraham 'Camped' in God's Promise

When Abraham, Sarah, and Lot came out of Egypt and returned to the land of Canaan, the blessings they had received from God became more than the land could contain. To avoid the dangerous snare of strife, Abraham offered Lot first choice of where he wanted to live. For Lot, this was where things took a turn for the worst.

Instead of building an altar with Abraham and praying for God's wisdom in the situation, Lot "...lifted up his eyes, and beheld all the plain of Jordan, that it was well watered every where, before the Lord destroyed Sodom and Gomorrah, even as the garden of the Lord, like the land of Egypt, as thou comest unto Zoar" (Genesis 13:10). Verse 11 says, "Then Lot chose him all the plain of Jordan; and Lot journeyed east: and they separated themselves the one from the other."

Meanwhile, Abraham stayed in the land of Canaan (*see* Genesis 13:12). Remember, Canaan was where God had called him; it was the land of promise. Thus Abraham *camped in God's promise*, trusting Him to honor His word and gift him the land as He had vowed to do.

From Lot's vantage point, he was able to see the beautiful Jordan Valley in the distance. He "beheld" it, which means he *carefully scrutinized it and viewed it with delight*. In that moment, he was hooked by what he saw. In many ways, the land was similar to the country of Ur from which he and Abraham had lived years earlier. Accordingly, he chose the plain of the Jordan and "...pitched his tent toward Sodom" (Genesis 13:12).

Sodom and Gomorrah Had a Reputation

If you carefully study the Scripture concerning this account, you will find numerous references to the cities of Sodom and Gomorrah. They are mentioned again and again from Genesis to Revelation.

Moses referred to Sodom and Gomorrah, saying, "...The whole land thereof is brimstone, and salt, and burning...which, the Lord overthrew in his anger, and in his wrath" (Deuteronomy 29:23). After the judgment of God, no vegetation that was planted there would sprout or grow.

Isaiah mentioned Sodom and Gomorrah several times, specifically citing that their sin was done shamelessly out in the open (*see* Isaiah 3:9).

Jeremiah told us that Sodom and Gomorrah were filled with adultery and lies (*see* Jeremiah 23:14).

Ezekiel said that Sodom and Gomorrah were filled with "pride, fullness of bread, and abundance of idleness" (Ezekiel 16:49). They disregarded the poor and needy, and instead were haughty and committed abominations in God's sight.

Amos warned other cities that if they didn't repent, they would be judged like Sodom and Gomorrah (*see* Amos 4:1-12).

Zephaniah notified Moab and Ammon that they would also be judged like Sodom and Gomorrah, which would turn their land into total desolation (*see* Zephaniah 2:9).

Even **Jesus** spoke about Sodom and Gomorrah on three different occasions. He said in Luke 17:28 and 29 that the people of Sodom were very affluent and prosperous. They ate, drank, bought, sold, planted, and built their lives as they saw fit. But God rained fire and brimstone down on them because of their sin. Jesus prophesied that the cities that heard His message but that would not repent would be judged more severely than Sodom and Gomorrah (*see* Matthew 10:15). He also predicted that cities like Capernaum that saw His mighty works and did not repent would be judged more severely than Sodom and Gomorrah (*see* Matthew 11:23,24).

The apostle **Paul** talked about a remnant of Israel being spared and not utterly destroyed like Sodom and Gomorrah (*see* Romans 9:29).

Peter declared that just as God destroyed Sodom and Gomorrah, a day is coming in the future when He is going to judge the wicked in like manner (*see* 2 Peter 2:4-11).

Jude told us that Sodom and Gomorrah gave themselves to fornication and went after strange flesh (*see* v. 7). The phrase "strange flesh" means the people of these cities were involved in *all kinds of sexual perversion, including homosexuality.*

Finally, when you come to the book of Revelation, **John** described Sodom as a symbol of sin and all defilement (*see* Revelation 11:7,8). Clearly, Sodom and Gomorrah were horribly wicked cities. They were so horrific that God wiped them off the face of the earth. Yet Sodom was the city that Lot pitched his tent toward. What in the world was this righteous man doing there?

Lot Was Mesmerized by Sodom

History tells us that the city of Sodom was a very wealthy and luxurious place — loaded with affluence and abundant business opportunities. It was actually the capital city of the region, which included the cities of Gomorrah, Admah, Zeboiim, and Zoar (*see* Genesis 14:2).

Initially, Lot lived outside the city on the plain of the Jordan Valley. However, with his tent pitched toward Sodom, its tantalizing allure was always in focus. From the confines of his tent he could see the city lights, hear its sounds, and smell the odor of revelry and celebration wafting through the air. Magnetically, Sodom's glamor pulled Lot closer and closer until he finally ended up living within the city itself (*see* Genesis 19:1-3).

In his heart, Lot knew he shouldn't have been in Sodom. The Bible says, "The men of Sodom were wicked and sinners before the Lord exceedingly" (Genesis 13:13). Yet he did what many believers do today — he coaxed and convinced himself into believing that what he was doing was acceptable. Little by little, he compromised his standards until he ended up in an evil, ungodly place and became totally backslidden from God.

The Lord Heard the Cry of Sodom's Sin

Genesis 18 records an extraordinary encounter Abraham experienced with the Lord. The Bible says, "The Lord appeared unto him in the plains of Mamre: and he sat in the tent door in the heat of the day (v. 1). The word "Lord" here is the word *Hashem*, which means *mercy*. Thus we could say that *Mercy* appeared to Abraham that day. Clearly, the Lord's appearing to Abraham was a very merciful act.

Verse 2 says that Abraham "...looked, and, lo, three men stood by him: and when he saw them, he ran to meet them from the tent door, and bowed himself toward the ground." From the full reading of this chapter, it's clear that two of these "men" were angels, and the third was the Lord God Himself.

After Abraham prepared and served the visitors a scrumptious meal, verses 16 and 17 say, "...The men rose up from thence, and looked toward Sodom: and Abraham went with them to bring them on the way. And the Lord said, Shall I hide from Abraham that thing which I do?" As noted at the opening of this lesson, the Lord and these angels had come from Heaven to investigate the severity of the sin in Sodom and to determine if it was as decadent as the cry they had heard.

There are two things noted in Scripture that take place on earth that God hears in Heaven. One is *the cry of His people*. Psalm 34:15 says, "The eyes of the Lord are upon the righteous, and his ears are open unto their cry." When God hears the cry of His people, He comes down to deliver them (*see* Psalm 34:17,19). The second thing God hears in Heaven is *the cry of sin*; the more grievous the sin, the louder the cry. Sin that is grievous gets God's attention, and He comes down to investigate it. Genesis 18:20-22 says, "The Lord said, Because the cry of Sodom and Gomorrah is great, and because their sin is very grievous, I will go down now, and see whether they have done altogether according to the cry of it, which is come unto me; and if not, I will know. And the men turned their faces from thence, and went toward Sodom: but Abraham stood yet before the Lord."

At that point, the Lord dispatched the two angels to go check out Sodom. Abraham knew Lot and his family were living there and that they were in trouble. Heaven had heard the cry of Sodom's sin, and now they were going to investigate it. Would it be as terrible as it had sounded? Would it be worse? In that moment, Abraham realized if he didn't make quick intercession, his nephew Lot — whom he deeply loved and believed was his only living heir — would be wiped away in the destruction.

Abraham Boldly Negotiated With the Lord

The Bible says, "Abraham drew near, and said, Wilt thou also destroy the righteous with the wicked?" (Genesis 18:23). Amazingly, Abraham called Lot, who was not living righteously, "righteous." He then proceeded to negotiate a deal with the Lord — a deal that would hopefully spare the city of judgment and thereby spare the lives of his nephew and his family.

> Peradventure there be fifty righteous within the city: wilt thou also destroy and not spare the place for the fifty righteous that are therein? That be far from thee to do after this manner, to slay the righteous with the wicked: and that the righteous should be as the wicked, that be far from thee: Shall not the Judge of all the earth do right? And the Lord said, If I find in Sodom fifty righteous within the city, then I will spare all the place for their sakes. And Abraham answered and said, Behold now, I have taken upon me to speak unto the Lord, which am but dust and ashes: Peradventure there shall lack five of the fifty righteous: wilt thou destroy all the city for lack of five? And he said, If I find there forty and five, I will not destroy it. And he spake unto him yet again, and said, Peradventure there shall be forty found there. And he said, I will not do it for forty's sake. And he said unto him, Oh let not the Lord be angry, and I will speak: Peradventure there shall thirty be found there. And he said, I will not do it, if I find thirty there. And he said, Behold now, I have taken upon me to speak unto the Lord: Peradventure there shall be twenty found there. And he said, I will not destroy it for twenty's sake. And he said, Oh let not the Lord be angry, and I will speak yet but this once: Peradventure ten shall be found there. And he said, I will not destroy it for ten's sake.
>
> — Genesis 18:24-32

Starting with 50 people and going down to 10, Abraham bargained with God, hoping He would spare the city even if there was only a small number of righteous living among them. More than likely, Abraham knew in advance that 10 was the number where he would stop. Most scholars agree that Lot, his wife, his children, and his sons-in-law probably totaled 10 in number. The reason Abraham went through the negotiation process was to carefully test the Lord and see how bold he could be.

God Wants You To Approach Him Boldly

Interestingly, when Abraham finished his negotiation with the Lord, the Bible says, "…The Lord went his way, as soon as he had left communing with Abraham: and Abraham returned unto his place" (Genesis 18:33). God was not angry or offended with Abraham. As far as the Lord was concerned, Abraham's bold intercession was high-level "communing," and He seemed to enjoy it.

Hebrews 4:16 instructs us to "…come boldly unto the throne of grace, that we may obtain mercy, and find grace to help in time of need." The word "boldly" is the Greek word *parresia*, which was used in ancient times to depict *one who spoke his mind and did it straightforwardly and with great confidence*. The Lord wants you to be bold and blunt when you come to Him in prayer — especially when you or someone else is in trouble.

When you do, you will "find grace to help in time of need." The word "find" is the Greek word *eurisko*, which means *to make a startling, unexpected discovery*. It is from where we get the word "eureka." This means that when you pray for people who are in trouble, you will come to a *eureka* moment — finding just what you need when you need it.

This brings us to the phrase "help in time of need." This phrase is from the Greek word *boetheia*, which was *a military word that depicted the moment when a soldier heard a fellow fighter was entrenched in battle, captured, or struggling — and once alerted to this situation, the soldier quickly went into battle to fight for the safety and well-being of his fellow fighter who was in trouble.*

If you know someone who's in trouble — someone who's making critically wrong decisions — rather than just sit and watch, *be bold in prayer!* Pray confidently and pray frankly. Be blunt with God and — *Eureka!* — you will find the answer to your prayer as Jesus, the Greatest Warrior of all, comes forward to deliver the one in trouble.

STUDY QUESTIONS

Study to shew thyself approved unto God, a workman that needeth
not to be ashamed, rightly dividing the word of truth.
— 2 Timothy 2:15

1. Sodom and Gomorrah are mentioned in more than a dozen books
   of the Bible by at least six prophets, four disciples, and Jesus Himself.
   What new insights did you learn about these cities and God's purpose
   for including them in Scripture?

2. As a child of God, it is vital that you know God hears you when you
   cry out to Him for help. Take a few minutes to meditate on Psalm
   34:15-20 and 145:18 and 19. What is the Holy Spirit speaking to you
   in these passages about His attentiveness to your cries for help? (Also
   consider 2 Samuel 22:7-10 and Psalm 18:6-9.)

PRACTICAL APPLICATION

But be ye doers of the word, and not hearers only,
deceiving your own selves.
— James 1:22

1. Who do you know who once walked with the Lord, but who is
   presently on the brink of destruction — totally blinded to his or her
   position and condition? What do you think caused that person to
   drift from the faith?

2. In addition to praying a covering of the blood of Jesus *over* that person
   and *against* the enemy, what specific things can you pray over his
   or her life? Are there any specific scriptures that come to mind that
   you can pray over that person? If so, which ones?

TOPIC

Lot: A Man Defeated by His Environment

SCRIPTURES

1. **Genesis 18:16,17** — And the men rose up from thence, and looked toward Sodom: and Abraham went with them to bring them on the way. And the Lord said, Shall I hide from Abraham that thing which I do?

2. **Genesis 18:20-33** — And the Lord said, Because the cry of Sodom and Gomorrah is great, and because their sin is very grievous, I will go down now, and see whether they have done altogether according to the cry of it, which is come unto me; and if not, I will know. And the men turned their faces from thence, and went toward Sodom: but Abraham stood yet before the Lord. And Abraham drew near, and said, Wilt thou also destroy the righteous with the wicked? Peradventure there be fifty righteous within the city: wilt thou also destroy and not spare the place for the fifty righteous that are therein? That be far from thee to do after this manner, to slay the righteous with the wicked: and that the righteous should be as the wicked, that be far from thee: Shall not the Judge of all the earth do right? And the Lord said, If I find in Sodom fifty righteous within the city, then I will spare all the place for their sakes. And Abraham answered and said, Behold now, I have taken upon me to speak unto the Lord, which am but dust and ashes. Peradventure there shall lack five of the fifty righteous: wilt thou destroy all the city for lack of five? And he said, If I find there forty and five, I will not destroy it. And he spake unto him yet again, and said, Peradventure there shall be forty found there. And he said, I will not do it for forty's sake. And he said unto him, Oh let not the Lord be angry, and I will speak: Peradventure there shall thirty be found there. And he said, I will not do it, if I find thirty there. And he said, Behold now, I have taken upon me to speak unto the Lord: Peradventure there shall be twenty found there. And he said, I will not destroy it for twenty's sake. And he said, Oh let not

the Lord be angry, and I will speak yet but this once: Peradventure ten shall be found there. And he said, I will not destroy it for ten's sake. And the Lord went his way, as soon as he had left communing with Abraham: and Abraham returned unto his place.

3. **Genesis 19:1-12** — And there came two angels to Sodom at even; and Lot sat in the gate of Sodom: and Lot seeing them rose up to meet them; and he bowed himself with his face toward the ground. And he said, Behold now, my lords, turn in, I pray you, into your servant's house, and tarry all night, and wash your feet, and ye shall rise up early, and go on your ways. And they said, Nay; but we will abide in the street all night. And he pressed upon them greatly; and they turned in unto him, and entered into his house; and he made them a feast, and did bake unleavened bread, and they did eat. But before they lay down, the men of the city, even the men of Sodom, compassed the house round, both old and young, all the people from every quarter. And they called unto Lot, and said unto him, Where are the men which came in to thee this night? bring them out unto us, that we may know them. And Lot went out at the door unto them, and shut the door after him. And said, I pray you, brethren, do not so wickedly. Behold now, I have two daughters which have not known man; let me, I pray you, bring them out unto you, and do ye to them as is good in your eyes: only unto these men do nothing; for therefore came they under the shadow of my roof. And they said, Stand back. And they said again, This one fellow came in to sojourn, and he will needs be a judge: now will we deal worse with thee, than with them. And they pressed sore upon the man, even Lot, and came near to break the door. But the men put forth their hand, and pulled Lot into the house to them, and shut the door. And they smote the men that were at the door of the house with blindness, both small and great: so that they wearied themselves to find the door. And the men said unto Lot, Hast thou here any besides? son in law, and thy sons, and thy daughters, and whatsoever thou hast in the city, bring them out of this place.

SYNOPSIS

Here one day and utterly destroyed the next. That was the fate of the cities of Sodom and Gomorrah. Archeological evidence from the southern region of the Dead Sea where these cities were once located reveals that sometime during the middle of the Twenty-First Century BC this area was overwhelmed by a great fire. Genesis 19:24 states, "The Lord rained upon Sodom and upon Gomorrah brimstone and fire from the Lord out of heaven." Yet in His mercy, before destruction came, the Lord gave His friend Abraham a forewarning of what He was about to do. God's conversation and interaction with him is recorded in Genesis 18, and it offers an example of how we, too, can intercede for people who are defeated by the ungodly environment in which they live.

The emphasis of this lesson:

Although Lot was a righteous man, he was not living righteously when he was in Sodom. The deceptiveness of sin had infiltrated his heart and perverted his mind, leaving him and his family corrupted and defeated.

A Heavenly Investigation Was Conducted

The Lord and two angels came down from Heaven to assess just how vile the sin of Sodom was. After taking time to partake of a meal prepared by Abraham, the Bible says, "The men rose up from thence, and looked toward Sodom: and Abraham went with them to bring them on the way. And the Lord said, Shall I hide from Abraham that thing which I do?" (Genesis 18:16,17.)

The Lord continued in verses 20 and 21, "…Because the cry of Sodom and Gomorrah is great, and because their sin is very grievous, I will go down now, and see whether they have done altogether according to the cry of it, which is come unto me; and if not, I will know." In effect, the Lord said, "Is this sin as bad as what we've heard? Because it is so grievous, we've come to investigate ourselves."

As we learned in the previous lesson, there are two cries that reach the Lord's ears in Heaven. First is *the cry of His people* who are in trouble. The cry of the children of Israel in Egyptian bondage is an example of this (*see* Exodus 3:7-9). Second is *the cry of sin*, and the sin of Sodom and Gomorrah is an example. The Lord hears and responds to both of these "cries."

Abraham Drew Near to the Lord

After the two angels were dispatched and began making their way toward Sodom, Abraham stood before the Lord and drew near Him with his concerns. Having heard the purpose of the Lord's visit, Abraham knew Lot and his family were in trouble. They were living in Sodom, and if it was about to be destroyed, Lot and all who were with him would be destroyed too. With a sense of urgency and reverential fear, Abraham began negotiating with the Lord:

> Peradventure there be fifty righteous within the city: wilt thou also destroy and not spare the place for the fifty righteous that are therein? That be far from thee to do after this manner, to slay the righteous with the wicked: and that the righteous should be as the wicked, that be far from thee: Shall not the Judge of all the earth do right? And the Lord said, If I find in Sodom fifty righteous within the city, then I will spare all the place for their sakes. And Abraham answered and said, Behold now, I have taken upon me to speak unto the Lord, which am but dust and ashes: Peradventure there shall lack five of the fifty righteous: wilt thou destroy all the city for lack of five? And he said, If I find there forty and five, I will not destroy it. And he spake unto him yet again, and said, Peradventure there shall be forty found there. And he said, I will not do it for forty's sake. And he said unto him, Oh let not the Lord be angry, and I will speak: Peradventure there shall thirty be found there. And he said, I will not do it, if I find thirty there. And he said, Behold now, I have taken upon me to speak unto the Lord: Peradventure there shall be twenty found there. And he said, I will not destroy it for twenty's sake. And he said, Oh let not the Lord be angry, and I will speak yet but this once: Peradventure ten shall be found there. And he said, I will not destroy it for ten's sake.
>
> — Genesis 18:24-32

Like an auctioneer working in reverse, Abraham haggled with God in hopes of sparing the city — even if there were only a small number from high to low of righteous people. He probably knew beforehand that ten was the number of people where he would stop. The consensus among most scholars is that Lot, his wife, his children, and his sons-in-law were about ten in number. The reason Abraham went through the negotiation process was to carefully test the Lord and see how bold he could be.

Hebrews 4:16 admonishes us to "...come boldly unto the throne of grace, that we may obtain mercy, and find grace to help in time of need." The word "boldly" is the Greek word *parresia*, which means *to be bold, frank,* or *blunt.* When you know someone is in trouble, you need to boldly take action. Rather than simply wringing your hands in worry, you need to draw near to the Lord in prayer and fearlessly intercede for his or her deliverance — just as Abraham did for Lot. Your intercession can snatch that person out of serious trouble.

Genesis 18:33 says, "And the Lord went his way, as soon as he had left communing with Abraham: and Abraham returned unto his place." God was not offended by Abraham's boldness; He called it *communion*. The fact that Abraham "returned unto his place" means he went home and went to bed. He felt he had sealed the safety of Lot and his family and was therefore totally at peace. You, too, can rest assured that God will help the people for whom you are praying. He will respond to your prayers just as He responded to Abraham.

The Angels Arrived in Sodom

Genesis 19:1 says, "And there came two angels to Sodom at even; and Lot sat in the gate of Sodom...." Note where Lot was sitting: *in the gate of Sodom*. This shows us how low he had sunk morally. For him to be at the city gate means he was a public official of some kind. The demented and perverted people of Sodom had elected him to serve as a city leader. There was something in Lot's character and behavior that the citizens saw and approved of. To some extent, he had become one of them.

Genesis 19:1 and 2 says, "...There came two angels to Sodom at even; and Lot sat in the gate of Sodom; and Lot seeing them rose up to meet them; and he bowed himself with his face toward the ground. And he said, Behold now, my lords, turn in, I pray you, into your servant's house, and tarry all night, and wash your feet, and ye shall rise up early, and go on your ways. And they said, Nay; but we will abide in the street all night."

Lot's invitation to stay at his place was more than just a gesture of hospitality. He knew what went on in Sodom during the night. The streets swarmed with all kinds of depraved, perverse sexual activity — including homosexuality. This was Sodom and it was filled with Sodomites. Lot didn't want the angels walking around the city at night unprotected. It is also possible that he was trying to protect the city from the angels bringing judgment on it.

After the angels rejected Lot's initial invitation, the Bible says, "He pressed upon them greatly; and they turned in unto him, and entered into his house; and he made them a feast, and did bake unleavened bread, and they did eat. But before they lay down, the men of the city, even the men of Sodom, compassed the house round, both old and young, all the people from every quarter: And they called unto Lot, and said unto him, Where are the men which came in to thee this night? bring them out unto us, that we may know them" (Genesis 19:3-5).

Men of all ages — both young and old — from every sector of the city surrounded the house and in a lustful rage demanded that the two visitors be brought out to them so that they could forcibly have sex with them. This lets us know that the sexual perversity was not confined to the adult generation alone; the young men were just as depraved.

Lot Became a Shadow of the Man He Once Was

Obviously, the angels who appeared in the form of men were the talk of the town — two new candidates that no one had yet "experienced." With their lust now burning out of control, the Sodomites' deviant intent was to gang-rape the angels. Knowing this, "Lot went out at the door unto them, and shut the door after him. And said, I pray you, brethren, do not so wickedly" (Genesis 19:6,7).

Notice what Lot called the men of Sodom: *brethren.* Keep in mind that this is the same Lot who once walked in faith with his Uncle Abraham. He had previously helped build altars to God and had seen God's mighty hand of protection, His hand of provision, and His hand of mercy. But being absent from God's presence and present in the perversion of Sodom had so twisted Lot's thinking that he was only a shadow of the man he once was. He had become so brainwashed by the atmosphere of Sodom that he stood before the Sodomites who wanted to rape the angels, and he called them "brethren."

"Don't do such a wicked thing," Lot said. Yet look in verse 8 at what he offered as a solution to the situation: "Behold now, I have two daughters which have not known man; let me, I pray you, bring them out unto you, and do ye to them as is good in your eyes: only unto these men do nothing; for therefore came they under the shadow of my roof."

If there was any question whether or not Lot had become a reprobate, his words in verse 8 answer it. The word "reprobate" is the Greek word *adokimos*, and it describes *a brain that is no longer normal, but greatly flawed; what was once created to be brilliant is no longer functioning the way it was intended.* Interestingly, Lot is called a "righteous" and "just" man in Second Peter chapter 2. Yet this righteous and just man had so defiled and seared his conscience that he had lost his sense of what was right and wrong. In his warped thinking, he had come to the conclusion that while it was wrong to rape his guests, it was acceptable to rape his daughters. No father in his right mind would ever think such a thing — *ever*.

When the Sodomites Pushed Back, the Angels Took Charge

Driven by lustful depravity, the men of Sodom responded to Lot, "Stand back!" Genesis 19:9 and 10 says, "…And they said again, This one fellow came in to sojourn, and he will needs be a judge: now will we deal worse with thee, than with them. And they pressed sore upon the man, even Lot, and came near to break the door."

In essence, the Sodomites told Lot, "Who in the world do you think you are? You of all people — are *you* going to judge us? Are *you* going to tell us what's right and what's wrong? Not a chance! When we're done with these two, we'll treat you even worse than them!"

Lot had so blended with the environment of Sodom that he had lost any voice of influence regarding morality. Any witness of truth and godliness he once possessed had disintegrated. He was now a Sodomite like them. Even if he was not involved in the acts of homosexuality, his thinking had become severely contaminated.

With things now escalating out of control, "…the men [angels] put forth their hand, and pulled Lot into the house to them, and shut the door. And they smote the men that were at the door of the house with blindness, both small and great: so that they wearied themselves to find the door" (Genesis 19:10,11).

Amazingly, even though the Sodomites had been blinded, they were so consumed with lust that they were still fighting to find the door so that they could get to the angels. The Lord used blindness to stop the men from getting to Lot and the angels and also to stop them from escaping the city before His judgment fell.

After the door was secured and Lot was inside, the two angels asked him, "Hast thou here any besides? son in law, and thy sons, and thy daughters, and whatsoever thou hast in the city, bring them out of this place" (Genesis 19:12).

It is interesting to note that Lot had *sons-in-law*, yet in a previous verse, it says that the two daughters with him had never "known a man." It is very possible that these two daughters were married to men with whom they had never had a sexual relationship. It may be that the men they married were active homosexuals, which is why the women never consummated their marriages with their husbands.

Remember Lot's Life!

Lot's life and that of his family is a picture of what happens when you abandon a life of faith. You may think you're "taking a break" from living a holy life or choosing an easier, less restrictive route that will get you to Heaven with no change in your present lifestyle. But in reality, the only thing you're doing is compromising your standards to accommodate your flesh and comfort your conscience.

If you find yourself being tempted to abandon what you know in your heart is right, please think again. Let Lot's example motivate you to seek the Lord for strength to stay the course on which He has placed you. Compromising will only lead to unwanted consequences. Obedience will lead to blessings!

STUDY QUESTIONS

Study to shew thyself approved unto God, a workman that needeth not to be ashamed, rightly dividing the word of truth.
— 2 Timothy 2:15

1. Lot's life is an example of what happens when we abandon a life of faith. What negative consequences can you identify from his example that you want to avoid in your own life?

2. There are many exciting blessings of walking in close relationship with the Lord, including *foreknowledge* of what is forthcoming. Take a few moments to meditate on this principle found in Amos 3:7; Psalm 25:14; John 16:13; and First Corinthians 2:9 and 10. What is the Holy Spirit showing you in these verses?

3. The Bible gives us a definition of pure, undefiled religion in the eyes of God in James 1:27. Take a moment and write out this threefold standard of holiness, paying close attention to the third aspect. (Also *consider* Psalm 24:3,4 and 2 Corinthians 7:1.)

PRACTICAL APPLICATION

But be ye doers of the word, and not hearers only,
deceiving your own selves.
— James 1:22

Lot is an example of a compromising Christian — one who yields to and accommodates his fleshly desires. Romans 13:14 (*J.B. Phillips*) says, "Let us be Christ's men from head to foot, and give no chances to the flesh to have its fling." Be honest with yourself and the Lord:

1. Is there a place in your life where you are giving in to your fleshly desires — accommodating and comforting your old sinful nature? If so, where?

2. Take time now to pray, asking God to forgive you and cleanse you of any thinking or behavior that has contaminated you, the temple of His Holy Spirit (*see* 2 Corinthians 3:16).

3. What practical steps can you take to *starve your flesh* and stop fueling the fire of impure desire?

4. In what specific ways can you *feed your spirit* the powerful, purifying truth of God's Word?

LESSON 4

TOPIC
Lot: A Righteous Man Who Wasn't Living Righteously

SCRIPTURES

1. **2 Peter 2:9** — The Lord knoweth how to deliver the godly out of temptations…

2. **Genesis 19:1-16** — And there came two angels to Sodom at even; and Lot sat in the gate of Sodom: and Lot seeing them rose up to meet them; and he bowed himself with his face toward the ground. And he said, Behold now, my lords, turn in, I pray you, into your servant's house, and tarry all night, and wash your feet, and ye shall

rise up early, and go on your ways. And they said, Nay; but we will abide in the street all night. And he pressed upon them greatly; and they turned in unto him, and entered into his house; and he made them a feast, and did bake unleavened bread, and they did eat. But before they lay down, the men of the city, even the men of Sodom, compassed the house round, both old and young, all the people from every quarter. And they called unto Lot, and said unto him, Where are the men which came in to thee this night? bring them out unto us, that we may know them. And Lot went out at the door unto them, and shut the door after him. And said, I pray you, brethren, do not so wickedly. Behold now, I have two daughters which have not known man; let me, I pray you, bring them out unto you, and do ye to them as is good in your eyes: only unto these men do nothing; for therefore came they under the shadow of my roof. And they said, Stand back. And they said again, This one fellow came in to sojourn, and he will needs be a judge: now will we deal worse with thee, than with them. And they pressed sore upon the man, even Lot, and came near to break the door. But the men put forth their hand, and pulled Lot into the house to them, and shut the door. And they smote the men that were at the door of the house with blindness, both small and great: so that they wearied themselves to find the door. And the men said unto Lot, Hast thou here any besides? son in law, and thy sons, and thy daughters, and whatsoever thou hast in the city, bring them out of this place. For we will destroy this place, because the cry of them is waxen great before the face of the Lord; and the Lord hath sent us to destroy it. And Lot went out, and spake unto his sons in law, which married his daughters, and said, Up, get you out of this place; for the Lord will destroy this city. But he seemed as one that mocked unto his sons in law. And when the morning arose, then the angels hastened Lot, saying, Arise, take thy wife, and thy two daughters, which are here; lest thou be consumed in the iniquity of the city. And while he lingered, the men laid hold upon his hand, and upon the hand of his wife, and upon the hand of his two daughters; the Lord being merciful unto him: and they brought him forth, and set him without the city.

GREEK WORDS

1. "deliver" — ῥύομαι (*rhuomai*): pictures a last-ditch effort to save someone who is on the brink of destruction; to snatch

2. "temptation" — πειρασμός (*peirasmos*): a temptation; adversity; trouble

SYNOPSIS

According to the historian Josephus, the cities of Sodom and Gomorrah were exceedingly wealthy and prosperous, but they had become proud in their hearts and unjust toward others. Locked in a mindset of self-importance, they developed a hatred for strangers and also began practicing all kinds of deviant sexual acts that were exceedingly wicked in God's eyes.

Accompanied by two angels, the Lord Himself came down to see if the sin was as wicked as its cry that had reached Heaven. As He stood and communed with Abraham, He dispatched the two angels to Sodom as night was falling. They knew that the darkness of night would reveal the true light of the city's sinful activities. Sure enough, what they saw confirmed that the region was ripe for God's wrath.

The emphasis of this lesson:

Lot's choice to live in Sodom contaminated him and his entire family. Although Peter called him righteous and just, his life did not show it. It was only by the earnest intercession of Abraham that Lot and his family were saved.

Lot Had Become a Key Leader in Sodom

Genesis 19:1 says, "And there came two angels to Sodom at even; and Lot sat in the gate of Sodom: and Lot seeing them rose up to meet them; and he bowed himself with his face toward the ground." These are the same two angels who had just fellowshipped with Abraham and the Lord. Upon their arrival in Sodom, they found Lot at the city gate.

In parts of the Asian world, those who sat at the gate of the city were the fathers or leaders of that city. They were the businessmen and public servants who carried out the necessary transactions to make the city successful and keep it moving forward. Since this was where Lot was, he had obviously become one of Sodom's key leaders. In other words, he was officially a Sodomite. Even if he wasn't participating in the perverse sexual sins of the city, he was an integral part of the city's fabric.

The Angels Were Urged To Stay in the Safety of Lot's Home

As soon as Lot saw the angels, he recognized that they were godly visitors and invited them to stay with him. He knew that the streets of Sodom would soon be filled with all kinds of sexual depravity, and he didn't want them subjected to such decadent immorality. But the angels declined Lot's invitation. They had come to carry out the Lord's commands — to make an inspection of the city and confirm the intensity of the sin being committed.

With great urgency, Lot "…pressed upon them greatly; and they turned in unto him, and entered into his house; and he made them a feast, and did bake unleavened bread, and they did eat" (Genesis 19:3). Then verse 4 says, "But before they lay down, the men of the city, even the men of Sodom, compassed the house round, both old and young, all the people from every quarter."

Notice that all men, both *young and old*, came from "every quarter" of the city. This indicates that the sexual depravity was everywhere and it had permeated men of all ages. The entire city had become twisted and defiled in their thinking, and they were now surrounding Lot's residence.

Lot Attempted To Deal With the Demands of the Deviant Sodomites

Genesis 19:5 says that the men of Sodom began yelling at Lot from the street, "…Where are the men which came in to thee this night? bring them out unto us, that we may know them." Keep in mind these men were called Sodomites, which is from where we get the term *sodomy*. They were actively involved in all kinds of deviant sexual activities, including homosexuality. When they said that they wanted to "know" the angels, it meant they wanted to have sex with them.

Apparently, to the sick men of Sodom, these angels who appeared as men were uncharted territory waiting to be explored. No one in town had been with them, and the Sodomites' intention was to gang-rape them through the night.

"And Lot went out at the door unto them, and shut the door after him. And said, I pray you, brethren, do not so wickedly" (Genesis 19:6,7).

As we noted in our last lesson, Lot called these wicked, perverse men "brethren." The fact that he identified himself with the men of Sodom as "brothers" indicates he had veered greatly from the walk of faith he once shared with Abraham.

The level of Lot's debasement is revealed even more in the alternative solution he offered in verse 8. He said, "Behold now, I have two daughters which have not known man; let me, I pray you, bring them out unto you, and do ye to them as is good in your eyes: only unto these men do nothing; for therefore came they under the shadow of my roof."

Lot Had Become a Reprobate

The best word to describe Lot at this point is "reprobate." It is from the Greek word *adokimos,* and it means *one that is unapproved* or *something that is broken.* It describes *a mind that has become so tainted it can no longer think correctly or discern what is right and wrong.* Interestingly, even believers can become reprobates, and Lot is a perfect example.

The human mind is a gift from God, and it is a marvelous creation. However, if one subjects the mind to seeing, hearing, and meditating on wrong things again and again and again, it can become so negatively impacted and calloused that it can no longer think correctly or discern what is right and what is wrong. That is what happened to Lot. Although he saw that raping the angels was wrong, he failed to see the extreme depravity in offering his daughters to be raped. The truth is, both acts were wicked, but Lot was unable to see it.

The Angels Struck the Sodomites With Blindness

After hearing Lot's response, the men of Sodom were enraged. Genesis 19:9 says, "And they said, Stand back. And they said again, This one fellow came in to sojourn, and he will needs be a judge: now will we deal worse with thee, than with them. And they pressed sore upon the man, even Lot, and came near to break the door."

In effect, the evil men snarled, "Who are you to judge us? Who are you to tell us what is right and what is wrong?" The implication is, they knew something about Lot's character that disqualified him from being a voice of morality. To them his words were empty and meaningless.

At that point, the angels inside Lot's house "…put forth their hand, and pulled Lot into the house to them, and shut the door. And they smote the men that were at the door of the house with blindness, both small and great: so that they wearied themselves to find the door" (Genesis 19:10,11). Even after being stricken with blindness, the men of Sodom were so driven by lust that they continued clawing to try to get to the angels inside.

God's Plan To Destroy Sodom Was Revealed to Lot

Immediately, the angels turned to Lot and said, "…Hast thou here any besides? son in law, and thy sons, and thy daughters, and whatsoever thou hast in the city, bring them out of this place. For we will destroy this place, because the cry of them is waxen great before the face of the Lord; and the Lord hath sent us to destroy it" (Genesis 19:12,13).

Responding to the angel's urgent instructions, "…Lot went out, and spake unto his sons-in-law, which married his daughters, and said, Up, get you out of this place; for the Lord will destroy this city…" (Genesis 19:14). The rest of that verse says, "…But he seemed as one that mocked unto his sons in law."

Interestingly, Lot had sons-in-law just outside his door. Apparently, they were in the crowd of men that had gathered around his house. When Lot relayed the warning of Sodom's pending destruction, his sons-in-law, in effect, laughed. They had never seen their father-in-law act so seriously or "preach" to them about righteousness, so they thought he was joking. Clearly, Lot had lost his moral voice.

The Bible says, "When the morning arose, then the angels hastened Lot, saying, Arise, take thy wife, and thy two daughters, which are here; lest thou be consumed in the iniquity of the city" (Genesis 19:15). According to this verse, Lot didn't want to leave. Therefore, the angels "hastened," or hurried, him along.

Verse 16 says, "While he lingered, the men laid hold upon his hand, and upon the hand of his wife, and upon the hand of his two daughters; the Lord being merciful unto him: and they brought him forth, and set him without the city." In other words, the angels dragged Lot, his wife, and his two daughters out of Sodom. The angels had been given orders by the Lord to spare their lives because of Abraham's intercession. Abraham had

successfully sealed their safety when he communed with the Lord. And that is what your prayers will do for someone who is in trouble.

The Lord Knows How To Deliver the Righteous

Second Peter 2:9 says, "The Lord knoweth how to deliver the godly out of temptations, and to reserve the unjust unto the day of judgement to be punished." In context with the previous verses, Peter was talking about the Lord's merciful deliverance of Lot from the city of Sodom. The word "deliver" is the Greek word *rhuomai*, and it describes *a last-ditch effort to save someone who is on the brink of destruction; to snatch away*. Hence, this verse could be translated, "The Lord knows how *to snatch* the godly out of temptations."

The word "temptations" is the Greek word *peirasmos*, which means *a temptation; adversity;* or *any kind of trouble*. Thus the Lord knows how to snatch the righteous out of any bad situation they find themselves in.

Maybe you know someone like Lot who isn't living righteously, but at some point in his past, he repented and made Jesus the Lord of his life. This verse tells us that God knows how to deliver such a one, even if he is on the brink of destruction.

Do you have a spouse, a child, a relative, or a close friend who has erred and drifted from his or her faith in Christ? This person was once on fire for the Lord, actively involved in ministry, studying the Word, praying in the Spirit, going to church, and flowing in the gifts of the Spirit — but now he is making moral decisions that you know are going to produce dreadful consequences.

Worrying about that person won't change anything, but your prayers will! If you will stand in faith and pray for those you are concerned about, God will deliver them for your sake.

STUDY QUESTIONS

Study to shew thyself approved unto God, a workman that needeth not to be ashamed, rightly dividing the word of truth.
— 2 Timothy 2:15

Abraham's intercession for Lot to be saved from Sodom's destruction wasn't the first time he had bailed Lot out of a mess. He had also rescued him some time earlier when he had been captured and taken hostage by King Chedorlaomer. Take a few moments to read this account in Genesis 14:1-24.

1. What stands out to you most about Abraham's efforts to rescue his nephew?

2. What differences do you see in the king of Sodom's treatment of Abraham and the way Melchizedek, king of Salem, treated him?

3. Where was Lot when he was first captured? Where did he go once Abraham rescued him? What does this say to you about Lot?

PRACTICAL APPLICATION

But be ye doers of the word, and not hearers only,
deceiving your own selves.
— James 1:22

1. When Lot warned his sons-in-law of the coming destruction of Sodom, they laughed at him and thought he was joking. How do your family and friends react when you share something about God? Do they take you seriously or do they think you're joking? What might you do to improve your spiritual credibility in their eyes?

2. Looking at Lot's character from the time he parted ways with Abraham to the time he was dragged out of Sodom by the angels, what is most alarming and disturbing to you? Why?

LESSON 5

TOPIC

Lot: A Man Delivered Because of Abraham's Intercession

SCRIPTURES

1. **2 Peter 2:6-9** — And turning the cities of Sodom and Gomorrah into ashes condemned them with an overthrow, making them an ensample unto those that after should live ungodly. And delivered just Lot, vexed with the filthy conversation of the wicked. For that righteous

man dwelling among them, in seeing and hearing, vexed his righteous soul from day to day with their unlawful deeds. The Lord knoweth how to deliver the godly out of temptations....

2. **Genesis 19:24,25,27-29** — Then the Lord rained upon Sodom and upon Gomorrah brimstone and fire from the Lord out of heaven. And he overthrew those cities, and all the plain, and all the inhabitants of the cities, and that which grew upon the ground. And Abraham gat up early in the morning to the place where he stood before the Lord. And he looked toward Sodom and Gomorrah, and toward all the land of the plain, and beheld, and, lo, the smoke of the country went up as the smoke of a furnace. And it came to pass, when God destroyed the cities of the plain, that God remembered Abraham, and sent Lot out of the midst of the overthrow, when he overthrew the cities in the which Lot dwelt."

GREEK WORDS

1. "turning… into ashes" — τεφρόω (*tephroo*): to completely reduce to ashes; to incinerate; Roman historian Dio Cassius used this word to describe the inner rim of Mount Vesuvius that was constantly growing brittle; from time to time the brittle ridge would collapse and crash down into the deep throat of the huge volcano; eventually the entire top of the mountain collapsed, settling into the throat of the volcano, and it disappeared under the ash of the volcano

2. "condemned" — κατακρίνω (*katakrino*): pictures the damning judgment or condemning sentence of a court

3. "overthrow" — καταστροφή (*katastrophe*): catastrophe; what happened to Sodom and Gomorrah was a catastrophic event

4. "ensample" — ὑπόδειγμα (*hupodeigma*): a sculptor's small-scale model of a statue or monument; before the sculptor made the larger, finished product, first he experimented on a small-scale model, which he meticulously worked on to make certain each measurement and dimension was correct; when the small scale was proportionally exact and met his stiff artistic requirements, he took that small scale model and amplified it into the real, final product; a prototype

5. "delivered" — ῥύομαι (*rhuomai*): pictures a last-ditch effort to save someone who is on the brink of destruction; to snatch

6. "just" — δίκαιος (*dikaios*): the New Testament word used most often for righteous or righteousness

7. "vexed" — **καταπονέω** (*kataponeo*): to wear out, to tire out, to break down, to torture; to bring to a place of total and complete exhaustion

8. "filthy conversation" — **ἀσελγείᾳ** (*aselgeia*) and **ἀναστροφή** (*anastrophe*): the word **ἀσελγείᾳ** (*aselgeia*) denotes unbridled living with an emphasis on sensuality; the word **ἀναστροφή** (*anastrophe*) denotes lifestyle or behavior; together they mean unbridled, outrageous, sensuous behaviors and lifestyles

9. "wicked" — **ἄθεσμος** (*athesmos*): lawless; out of place; displaced morally

10. "righteous" — **δίκαιος** (*dikaios*): the New Testament word used most often for righteous or righteousness

11. "dwelling" — **ἐγκατοικέω** (*egkatoikeo*): to reside; pictures one who settles into a home and feels comfortable there

12. "vexed" — **βασανίζω** (*basanidzo*): the Greek word for torture

13. "soul" — **ψυχή** (*psuche*): the soul; the emotional and mental realm

14. "unlawful" — **ἄνομος** (*anomos*): without law; lawless, or having no moral standard; pictures people who possess no fixed moral standards; void of standards; living in a state of lawlessness

15. "deeds" — **ἔργον** (*ergon*): actions, deeds, or activities; a word so all-encompassing that it pictures actions, conducts, and beliefs

16. "knoweth" — **οἶδα** (*oida*): to see, perceive, understand, or comprehend; knowledge gained by personal experience or personal observation

17. "temptation" — **πειρασμός** (*peirasmos*): a temptation; adversity; trouble

SYNOPSIS

As we have noted, Sodom and Gomorrah were located in the Jordan Valley in what is now the southern end of the Dead Sea. A fault line runs through this region and forms the valley, which has been the scene of numerous earthquakes throughout history. The Bible says, "The Lord rained upon Sodom and Gomorrah brimstone and fire from the Lord out of heaven; and he overthrew those cities, and all of the plain, and all the inhabitants of the cities, and that which grew upon the ground" (Genesis 19:24,25).

It's understood that the Lord utilized the geological activity of the region to bring about its annihilation. A great earthquake coupled with a violent explosion served to propel fiery sulfur and salt into the sky. Interestingly, Josephus notes that the ruins of these cities were still visible and not yet covered by water in his day — in early New Testament times — more than 2,000 years after the event took place.

The emphasis of this lesson:

Lot was spared when the Lord destroyed the cities of Sodom and Gomorrah — even though he didn't want to leave — as a result of Abraham's prayers. This demonstrates the power of prayer and includes your prayers for people who need deliverance from coming destruction.

Sodom and Gomorrah Were Incinerated

The apostle Peter offers a striking commentary on Lot and the judgment of God that fell on Sodom and Gomorrah. Starting in Second Peter 2:6, it says, "And turning the cities of Sodom and Gomorrah into ashes condemned them with an overthrow, making them an ensample unto those that after should live ungodly."

To grasp the fullness of what is being communicated, we need to understand the original Greek meaning of the phrase "turning the cities of Sodom and Gomorrah into ashes." This is the Greek word *tephroo*, which means *to completely reduce to ashes; to incinerate*. Thus, this verse could be translated, "God *incinerated* Sodom and Gomorrah, *completely reducing them to ashes*."

Interestingly, the Greek word *tephroo* was used by Roman historian Dio Cassius to describe the inner rim of Mount Vesuvius that was constantly growing brittle. From time to time, the brittle ridge would collapse and crash down into the deep throat of the huge volcano; eventually the entire top of the mountain collapsed, settling into the throat of the volcano, and it disappeared under the ash of the volcano.

The word *tephroo* is the same word Peter used to describe what happened to Sodom and Gomorrah. The ground where these cities were located became so brittle, just like the rim of Mount Vesuvius, it eventually collapsed, settled into the earth, and disappeared. This took place in what is today the southern end of the Dead Sea. It is the lowest point on the face of the Earth — approximately 1,290 feet below sea level. It serves as a living memorial of God's judgment of sin.

They Serve As an Example
of God's Coming Judgment

Peter also said that God "condemned" Sodom and Gomorrah. The word "condemned" is the Greek word *katakrino*, which is a compound of two words: *kata*, which describes *something coming down*, and the word *krino*, which means *to judge*. When these two words are combined to form the word *katakrino*, it pictures *the damning judgment or condemning sentence of a court*. Heaven put Sodom and Gomorrah and the cities of the plain on trial and ruled that they didn't deserve to exist any longer, Accordingly, God condemned them and they were overthrown.

Next is the word "overthrow," which is the Greek word *katastrophe*, and it describes a *catastrophe* just as it sounds. What happened to Sodom and Gomorrah was a catastrophic event, and it serves as an "ensample," which is the Greek word *hupodeigma*, and would better be translated as *example*.

The interesting backstory on this word *hupodeigma* ("ensample") is *that it described a sculptor's small-scale model of a statue or monument*. Before the sculptor made the larger, finished product, first he experimented on a small-scale model, which he meticulously worked on to make certain each measurement and dimension was correct. When the small scale was proportionally exact and met his stiff artistic requirements, he took that small-scale model and amplified it into the real, final product. Thus, the word *hupodeigma* describes *a prototype*.

The destruction of Sodom and Gomorrah was God's *prototype* of the judgment that is coming in the future. In other words, before God creates the full-scale version of His final judgement against sin, He made the small-scale model of Sodom and Gomorrah to confirm that everything meets His requirements. It serves as a vivid picture of what is going to happen to the ungodly in the future.

Righteous Lot Was Vexed By Filthy Conversation

The New Testament commentary on Lot and the judgment of God on Sodom and Gomorrah continues in Second Peter 2:7. It says, "And delivered just Lot, vexed with the filthy conversation of the wicked." The word "just" is the Greek word *dikaios*, which is *the New Testament word used most often for righteous or righteousness*. Despite his decision to live in Sodom amidst all kinds of sexual sin and perversity, God saw Lot as *righteous*.

And God "delivered" him. We saw in an earlier lesson that the word "delivered" is the Greek word *rhuomai*, and it pictures *a last-ditch effort to save someone who is on the brink of destruction*. It also means *to snatch*. A better translation of this verse would be, "God *snatched* righteous Lot, who was vexed with the filthy conversation of the wicked."

This brings us to the word "vexed," which is the Greek word *kataponeo*. This word gives us valuable insight into the kind of life Lot was living. *Kataponeo*, translated here as "vexed," means *to wear out, to tire out, to break down, to torture; to bring to a place of total and complete exhaustion*. Thus, living in the middle of the sin of Sodom "vexed" Lot greatly — it wore him out, broke him down, and brought him to a place of total exhaustion.

What was he specifically *vexed* by? The Bible says "filthy conversation." The word "filth" is the Greek word *aselgeia*, and it always denotes *unbridled living with an emphasis on sensuality*. The word "conversation" is the Greek word *anastrophe*, and it denotes *lifestyle or behavior*. When *aselgeia* and *anastrophe* and put together ("filthy conversation"), they describe *unbridled, outrageous, sensual behaviors and lifestyles*. This is a vivid picture of the people of Sodom and Gomorrah.

Scripture says the *filthy conversation* was coming from the "wicked," which in this verse is the Greek word *athesmos*. It describes *lawless people; people who are out of place or displaced morally*. These are individuals who are morally confused and no longer living by what is right. To a great degree, this is what we see in society today. Many people have rejected the law of God and are living *lawlessly*. They are morally confused, and as a result they are doing things that are incorrect and out of place. That is what the word *athesmos* (wicked) means.

Little by Little, Lot Calloused His Soul to Sin

Second Peter 2:8 goes on to say, "For that righteous man dwelling among them, in seeing and hearing, vexed his righteous soul from day to day with their unlawful deeds." Again, this verse declared Lot as "righteous" — the same Greek word *dikaios*, which is translated "just" in verse 6. It is the New Testament word for *righteous or righteousness*. Although Lot wasn't living righteously, he had dedicated his life to the Lord earlier, and therefore God called him righteous.

He was "dwelling" with the wicked. The word "dwelling" is the Greek word *egkatoikeo*, and it means *to reside*. It pictures *one who settles into a home and feels comfortable there.* Lot had become comfortable and at home in the environment of sin.

Again, the Bible says Lot was "vexed." However, the word "vexed" here is different than the word "vexed" in verse 7. It is the Greek word *basanidzo*, which means *torture.* Lot was *tortured* in his "soul," which is the Greek word *psuche*, and it refers to *the emotional and mental realm.* How did he torture his soul? Verse 8 says, "In seeing and hearing" the activities of Sodom. The tense in the Greek actually means, "In seeing and seeing and seeing; in hearing and hearing and hearing." It pictures an ongoing activity.

When you first see or hear about atrocious sin, it deeply grieves your heart. However, if you *see it* and *hear it* again and again and again, it will no longer grieve you as it did at first. Little by little, you will adapt to it and become calloused — or hardened — in your soul (your mind and emotions). That is what Lot did; he calloused his righteous soul by repeatedly seeing and hearing the deep depravity of Sodom.

In some situations, a person's soul becomes so calloused, he becomes a participant in the sin. For example, there are some Christians who once refused to watch movies with sex scenes and profanity in them, as it grieved their hearts deeply. Over time, however, they watched so many movies sprinkled with these types of things that they can now sit and view what used to grieve them deeply, and it doesn't bother them one bit. In fact, they don't even give it a second thought. Why? It's a result of callousing their heart. This shows us just how vital it is to guard what we're seeing and hearing each day and to stay away from ungodly things.

Specifically, Lot vexed his righteous soul with "unlawful deeds." The word "unlawful" is the Greek word *anomos*, which means *without law; lawless, or having no moral standard.* It pictures *people who possess no fixed moral standards.* They are void of standards, living in a state of lawlessness. Instead of living by the Word of God, they are living by their own concocted version of right and wrong.

The word "deeds" in this verse is the Greek word *ergon*, which describes *actions, deeds, or activities.* It is a word so all-encompassing that it pictures *actions, conducts, and beliefs.* The people of Sodom were doing wicked, unlawful deeds, and they actually believed it was all right. Why? It was the result of lawless living. They had no righteous standard; they were living by their own "politically-correct" standards.

The Lord Knows How To Deliver the Godly

Thankfully, that Bible says, "The Lord knoweth how to deliver the godly out of temptations…" (2 Peter 2:9). In God's mercy, Lot was delivered from the mess of Sodom. Again, we see the word "deliver" — the Greek word *rhuomai*, which pictures *a last-ditch effort to save someone who is on the brink of destruction*; it means *to snatch*.

Lot was living in the midst of "temptations." The word "temptations" is the Greek word *peirasmos*, which describes *a temptation; adversity*; or *trouble*. The Lord "knoweth" how to deliver the godly from any form of trouble. The word "knoweth" here is the Greek word *oida*, which means *to see, perceive, understand, or comprehend*. It is *knowledge gained by personal experience or personal observation*.

When we combine the meanings of all these words, this verse would better be translated, *"The Lord understands and fully comprehends from personal experience and observation how to snatch those who are on the brink of disaster — particularly, godly people who are not living very godly."*

God Remembered Abraham, and He Will Remember You!

Immediately after the angels dragged Lot, his wife, and his two daughters outside of Sodom, the Bible says, "The Lord rained upon Sodom and upon Gomorrah brimstone and fire from the Lord out of heaven. And he overthrew those cities, and all the plain, and all the inhabitants of the cities, and that which grew upon the ground. And Abraham gat up early in the morning to the place where he stood before the Lord" (Genesis 19:24,25,27).

Early in the morning, the day after the Lord's visitation, Abraham returned to the place where he had interceded on Lot's behalf. He had slept through the night, trusting that God would honor His word and deliver Lot and his family.

Verse 28 says, "And he looked toward Sodom and Gomorrah, and toward all the land of the plain, and beheld, and, lo, the smoke of the country went up as the smoke of a furnace." Remember, God incinerated Sodom and Gomorrah and the other wicked cities of the plain. They were gone. All that remained was the rising smoke.

One of the most important points of this teaching is found in Genesis 19:29. It says, "And it came to pass, when God destroyed the cities of the plain, that *God remembered Abraham*, and sent Lot out of the midst of the overthrow, when he overthrew the cities in the which Lot dwelt."

Remember, neither Lot nor his wife wanted to leave Sodom. Their identity was in Sodom. Their prestige was in Sodom. Their financial prosperity was in Sodom. After hesitating and lingering in the city all night, the angels grabbed Lot and his whole family by the hand and forced them out. Why? Because God remembered Abraham and the prayers he had prayed for his nephew.

Friend, don't underestimate the power of your prayers! If you will draw near to God and intercede for the person you know is in trouble, God will hear and He will answer. Whether it's your spouse, your child, your relative, your friend, your coworker, or someone else you know who has strayed from his faith in Christ, making decisions that are detrimental to his well-being, *pray!* God will move on that person's behalf for your sake. Just as God remembered Abraham, He will remember you!

STUDY QUESTIONS

Study to shew thyself approved unto God, a workman that needeth not to be ashamed, rightly dividing the word of truth.
— 2 Timothy 2:15

1. Abraham's prayers for Lot and his family literally saved their lives. Your prayers are just as powerful and vital in the lives of others. Carefully read James 5:16-20. What is the Lord showing you in this passage regarding the impact of your prayers — especially on those who wander from the faith? (Also *consider* Matthew 21:21,22; 1 John 5:14,15; and Jude 1:22,23.)

2. In your own words, briefly describe the process of callousing your soul to sin.

3. In what area(s) of your life have you experienced this progression?

4. What practical steps can you take to guard yourself from becoming calloused, or hardened, to sin? For some godly insight, read Psalm 101:1-4 and Second Corinthians 6:14-18.

PRACTICAL APPLICATION

But be ye doers of the word, and not hearers only,
deceiving your own selves.
— James 1:22

1. If you recognize that you have become calloused to sin, pray and ask the Lord to give you a new heart. Take a few moments to meditate on Ezekiel 36:26 and 27 and turn it into a brief, personal prayer request to God. (Also *consider* Psalm 51:1-3,10-12 and Ezekiel 11:19,20.)

2. One of the greatest safeguards you can have against becoming comfortable in an environment of sin is the *fear of the Lord*. Proverbs 16:6 (*AMPC*) declares, "...By the reverent, worshipful fear of the Lord men depart from and avoid evil." Make this attribute and work of the Holy Spirit a regular part of your requests to God. Pray, "Holy Spirit, please fill me with the Spirit of the Fear of the Lord, that I may delight in and be blessed by it, just as Jesus was" (*see* Isaiah 11:2,3).

A Prayer To Receive Salvation

If you've never received Jesus as your Savior and Lord, now is the time for you to experience the new life Jesus wants to give you! To receive God's gift of salvation that can be obtained through Jesus alone, pray this prayer from your heart:

Jesus, I repent of my sin and receive You as my Savior and Lord. Wash away my sin with Your precious blood and make me completely new. I thank You that my sin is removed, and Satan no longer has any right to lay claim on me. Through Your empowering grace, I faithfully promise that I will serve You as my Lord for the rest of my life.

If you just prayed this prayer of salvation, you are born again! You are a brand-new creation in Christ! Would you please let us know of your decision by going to **renner.org/salvation**? We would love to connect with you and pray for you as you begin your new life in Christ.

Scriptures for further study: John 3:16; John 14:6; Acts 4:12; Ephesians 1:7; Hebrews 10:19,20; 1 Peter 1:18,19; Romans 10:9,10; Colossians 1:13; 2 Corinthians 5:17; Romans 6:4; 1 Peter 1:3

Notes

_____

_____

_____

_____

_____

_____

_____

_____

_____

_____

_____

_____

_____

_____

_____

_____

_____

_____

_____

_____

_____

_____

_____

_____

_____

_____

_____

_____

_____

Notes

Notes

CLAIM YOUR FREE RESOURCE!

As a way of introducing you further to the teaching ministry of Rick Renner, we would like to send you FREE of charge his teaching, "How To Receive a Miraculous Touch From God" on CD or as an MP3 download.

In His earthly ministry, Jesus commonly healed *all* who were sick of *all* their diseases. In this profound message, learn about the manifold dimensions of Christ's wisdom, goodness, power, and love toward all humanity who came to Him in faith with their needs.

☑ **YES, I want to receive Rick Renner's monthly teaching letter!**

Simply scan the QR code to claim this resource or go to: **renner.org/claim-your-free-offer**

Connect

WITH US!

www.ingramcontent.com/pod-product-compliance
Lightning Source LLC
Chambersburg PA
CBHW071647040426
42452CB00009B/1790